Folks Like Me

To

Harry + Michael

from

Dan Carnott

1993

+ Folks like me

(John Ford
Jerry Goldsmith etc)

Books by Sam Cornish

Your Hand in Mine (Children)
Generations (Poetry)
Grandmother's Pictures (Children)
Sam's World (Poetry)
Songs of Jubilee (Poetry)
1935 (Memoir)

Folks Like Me

Sam Cornish

𝒵
ZOLAND BOOKS
Cambridge, Massachusetts

Some of these poems have previously been published in *Ploughshares, Kenyon Review, Emerson Review, Arion's Dolphin*, and in *1935* (published by Ploughshares Books).

First Edition

Printed in the United States of America

This book is printed on acid-free paper, and its binding materials have been chosen for strength and durability.

Book design by Boskydell Studio

Library of Congress Cataloging-in-Publication Data

Cornish, Sam.
    Folks like me : poems / by Sam Cornish.—1st ed.
      p.   cm.
    ISBN 0-944072-30-5 (acid-free paper) :
    1. Afro-Americans—History—Poetry. I. Title.
PS3553.068F6   1993
811'.54—dc20   92-43940
                                   CIP

For Ruth Whitman

The author provides grateful acknowledgment to the following periodicals in which some of these poems have appeared: *Ploughshares, Kenyon Review, Emerson Review, Arion's Dolphin* and *1935*, a book published by Ploughshares Books.

The author wishes to acknowledge the professional assistance, including editorial consultation and archival assistance, of FLAR. Thanks also to DeWitt Henry and the faculty of Writing and Publishing at Emerson College.

CONTENTS

Folks Like Me

Perfect Day

These women tell another story, of the good old days, when men in job lines were just sitting, of mothers paying college tuition, with a shopping bag full of nickels and dimes, husbands leaving after the third or fourth child, husbands marrying women who dismissed the Woman Warrior (the myth of the woman raising her children in the single family household). These women speak of the domestic maid who had spent her life with the (white) family (whom she never admired) and some of these households thought the maid—or at least they said—was family. The young children missed her when she left, even though they—in Southern families where the care of the maids and field workers were seen as obligations—visit often, send letters, call and come over and are expected by those former maids and mamas to be there at the door someday, if not today, with freshly caught fish, a few dollars, a gift or loan. These were white women who cannot understand the sit-ins or Jesse Jackson and should be told that these poems and writings are dedicated to Southern women . . . black women, white women. My mother did day work, my grandmother was a domestic.

General

Harriet Tubman is General Moses
Moses is coming
let the moon
        rise
for the Lord
Moses is coming
(I have been waiting
        for a new day)
Moses is coming
heard her stomping
the darkness
        coming to set
her children free

Sojourner

Wandering woman
struck down
in the sun
on that long and miserable
road

1.
ain't I a
woman
(but do I want
to be lifted
into carriages)   or
rather pull
like Harriet (a mighty beast)
my people   through the forest
    forge those mighty rivers

Mississippi
river of death
Ohio
river of the new
African peoples

2.
what do white
women
see when they think
of me   speak those words I spoke

(they
recite and perform) but never wrote
    ain't I a woman

Why I Did Not Give My Seat To
That White Man in 1932

I am a working woman
an all
day woman
my hands are stones
that beat
these clothes to white
sweat burns
my hips
churn and thrust
my breasts
have weaned
the South
my feet kept
moving long
after sun
rise and the moon
followed
me my old feet
my old feet
buried within my shoes
my head
is a southern tongue
my heart is the Scottsboro
boy   telling
his story
a tale longer
than the history
this woman has seen before she came home back
in the Jim Crow car

Horseface

Horseface
was so dark they
called her purple she
appeared at dances
without a date
she sat and stood
feet keeping time
silent and alone
little Mary (Horseface)
stroked her hair and sighed
little Mary so
black her skin
sings and shines
so black they talk
behind her back
oh she was so
black her father
passed out
(he wanted to lighten
the race) my wife did
this to me he said and left without a word said
it must be some nigger blacker than
me
little Mary
to me (Horseface
to some black
Mary to others)
stood on the road waved
at trains (maybe daddy is passin through) ran
toward cars making dust
in the afternoons sought
love from people going North
as her father did
somewhere lighter
someplace better

Honky Tonk

This is where the music comes from:
side streets   back
street Negro   blues
at the back door knocking
music of Satchmo
(Satch mouth)
church people
hustlers
old folks
shanty people
blues   standing
like   hard times
in my horn

preachers   with
"a handful of gimme"
& their slippery
hands
live in my horn

my mother a rough neck
busting heads
for a pair of shoes
these people   the music
in my horn

America As A Cabin

When America was not
America: a chest
of tea tossed
into the harbor
and slaves
black and indentured (white)
language of free men   words
a war of taxes   boxes of tea
tossed in Boston Harbor
the language
of free men black men talking
of white men and women   who knew
America as cabin   the mule
laboring   the bullwhip)   facing
a hostile
wood (an endless darkness pointing
north   of red men
talking water   laughing
buffalo   the promised land
of a common man   something
new   something white

Christian Hair

Free men are not
free Negroes
God of Christian men
speaks to the blacks
(head like a holler tree)
talking to rivers
calling the rabbit
the buzzard
the bear
brother

Workers of The Soil

I am a Negro worker   these
are my hands   (like marching feet)
the hands   of a working Negro
not an educated   man
but worker of the soil   the south land
is a hunger in my body   now thin
and early   to the street looking
for work   these are the   words
of   an undetected man
a working man
a Negro man

Ma

You heard
of Ma
Rainey
she made
the blues
sound
like a piano
moaning

Riot

In Chicago
after *Birth of a Nation*
and riots   wondering
if we would live
or see another summer
my teachers   those somber ladies
who read Claude McKay
looked deeply
into my eyes

If The Negro Cannot See Work As Honorable

The blind have
a dream
some say it's jazz
and booze   but Booker
T. Washington
Who never rode the Jim
Crow car
if he could   after all, he was a mulatto
some dream of sweet mamas
with firm buttocks
laughing mouths and slender
knowing fingers
but Booker T.
like a woman
naked in the troubled
Christian dark, trembled
and blushed as mulattos
do   looked at the shameless middle class learning Latin
instead of repairing a creaking gate or ploughing
and hoeing

Pauli Murray

Not being a gentleman
a lady
born
wearing   Proud Shoes
Mr. Roosevelt regrets:

the road gang
and shanty town   your mother looking
like a scarecrow

D.W. Griffith Elegy

After that still and gentle time
when my father
carried a sword and I a memory
of when the South rode to scare the darkness (and the slaves)
it was Lincoln and never Robert E. Lee
I admired and when (in my film *Birth
of a Nation*) Negroes were tossed
into the sea and the overseer laid bare their backs
with a lash they cut my film   the North remembers whites in black
face and Lillian Gish pure but sweet the nigger in the shadows with
his chicken and his lust my hero
(in some secret part of me where all men are white in the soul)
finds me in some gentle time
when I am Thoreau, Dickens and the women pure and driven
as the snow

Elegy

Old Folks before the break
o' day
kindle
a fire
a song for old
folks
and end of day
an elegy for those
gone and about
to go
old
folks like you
and me
a tune
upon the fiddle
to set
the feet to steppin
high and full
of life
(fresh as a new
morning)
that breakin
in a day like I
never see
before

kindle
a fire
in my soul
for Booker T.
a song
before
the break o'
day
a tune
now
when the breeze
is sighin

and the old
folks feel
like home
when the
sun is sittin
and the day
is put to rest
when the weary
thank
the mornin
praise the dusk
praise the Lord
and face
the dark   kindle a fire
strike a tune
for Mr. Washington
he made us proud
of pitch forks and brown
skins hard
work instead
of fine clothes
fit for opera
and not
for work
I think
of the poems
of field
songs about
the house the folk
at home
you
and me
(and the
little feller)
how Booker T.
taught
us to love
the land

to be
proud of the
work
of these hands
that work   hands
black   man black
woman strong family
workin

My Darkness Burns the Cross

Where you have died
for me
burns Lord
in my backyard
you have died for me
and the children
of Ham
you have made the day
stand still
waters rise and divide
for the Hebrew children
but Lord
this is Ms. Sarah's prayer
for the troubled
men of my race
full of pancakes booze and blues
with penis thick as
maple trees
afraid to trust a woman
mind full of book learning
lord these men
hung from trees (strange fruit)
dusky birds
Lord these are the sons
of slaves taught
to read whipped but defiant
this generation
disturbed by their blackness
drinking white lightning
the deep South in my bathroom
blind from lighting
made at home
dead from booze and the urban
night Lord you have never
been mean to me
although you don't
listen you have been
a light in my darkness

(blood filling
his father's
shoes)
living in a hollow
tree
(skin mangled
by dogs)
called the children
honey (although a slave)
old
black man born
before Jim Crow)
telling stories about
an American forest
Uncle Remus is not
your name
Uncle
Remus sings
America: tales
of the Southern
Woods
Joel Chandler Harris
heeded (ears bending)
the Negro people
(the overseer elsewhere)
(called runways
or just Negroes)
they knew cowhides
& sticks
the blood
of the old
man
is his stories

Not Long For The Day

Southern men   black men   Negro
men: learn
the clear language   of a life
sentenced to death
       how long   not long Haywood Patterson
       freedom train bit the dust

in prison   (Where Mohammed teaches)
the Negro is dark
skin a mouth   full and eager
to sing blues   & re-bop

Angelo Herndon
Lenin Marxist
Negro writing
quiet autobiography
wrote his book
from jail
three black men
King Kong striding
the rails might
think we're not long for the day
these black men   southern men
Negro northern African-American
men

Coke Bottle Glasses

As Coltrane sings
to some and holy
rollers heat
up the soul
for Jesus

Karl Marx
Frederick Engels
sustains me
I a Negro
"find a world"
my comrades
demanded
in 1932
as white   unemployed
joined the Black Shirts
the Knights
the Klan (the Christian
nation marches
in step
with America)
rides
bitterly
conveys
America
for
Americans

Negro Enough for Me

Walter White is Negro Enough For Me
Walter White did not have to live
as a Negro but he chose
to   let the world know
and   became an unwary black
man   after all race
is not a color
thought
Walter   it is a man
               and the man is me
Walter
White

Walter White

Imagine(ing) that this man wanted
to be   a Negro   Walter
could arrive in a Southern
town and hear
the white folk say   there is a nigger
        in town (nice
        and brown or speaking
        his mind)
Walter shakes   his straight (and good
deceptive head
of hair)   Negro blood
invisible but
running   (like a runaway)
        one eye gone   toe
        missing   getting on   dark
        of history and anger
this (my man's) man
a lawyer
looking white
and thinking colored ain't
all bad)

Walter White   the name
(white) does
not do him justice

Have You Heard the Little Presbyterian Children Sing

Have you heard the little
Presbyterian children sing
such dignity
dressed and starched
in gowns
of black
and white
little girls wearing
gloves
little ladies
on Sundays
brats
all week   ask their teacher
and those boys fine
and dressed like little undertakers
black suits and shoes
white shirts and socks
when they stand and sing proud as the finest house
giving welcome
to Sunday morning
little brown and black boys and girls
praising the morning   listen to them sing

Southern Sisters

Black Carol   blacker Miss
   Cora   sisters from the South   lived
in three rooms
in my mother's house   were
evil nasty and full
of jive   the men on Pennsylvania
said because they put their
money in the collection
plate and people
   made them so
washed my brother's
shirts until they were as white
   as ivory
soap combed my hair
with gentle brown fingers (and I didn't holler and moan)
black Carol and blacker Miss
Cora (stuck up like yellow gals)   called the rocking chair women
   at People's
   Baptist praising
on Sunday (rock back and forth)
   their shining black
   faces full
of grace
praise
   the Lord
ain't
   He grand

Preacher's Yellow Son

       Those yellow and proper boys
your mother said you should be like stole
       illustration
board from the art supply store those preacher's sons
always getting into trouble   stealing chickens   loving
Jelly Roll   being yellow   acting like a fool
       jitterbugging
       calling it
       rock and roll
cutting a rug doing the mashed potato
preacher swing your yellow hips
shake it preacher's son
so early in the morning and feeling no pain

Sunday Morning

Here comes
the band the marching
feet.
The neighbors, friends and shopkeepers stand
up and down the street.
Look at what the drum majorette can do.
John Philip Sousa is
deep somewhere in the drum.
The marching feet—
this ain't the Saturday night blues
but the Sunday morning parade.
Drumbeats loud
over the bar and dinner
table—the church pews are emptied out.
Drumbeats:
those fine colored boys and girls
old colored men
dressed in white
Sunday morning—
those proud marching feet
coming down the street.

Eddie Loves Little Lulu

Eddie is a laugh and fine shoes
full lips and white
teeth grinning
to high heaven
Eddie from Georgia   sorrowful place
        for a Negro
lived in one room   played numbers keeping the figures in his head
Eddie was sweet smelling life Dixie peach and after shave
handsome as
        a preacher suit and as dark   never
attended People's Baptist
God made Sunday
for fried chicken
reading the comic pages
of the *Baltimore Sun*

While Lincoln is Still Thinking

They baked the bread
bless their souls
raised children
broke the ground
like a plough
were the people
(no melting pot
farthest down)
they built the houses
shod the horses
they were the people
thousands gone
they sang
oh give Jesus
in that morning
when the lamp
burns low
run nigger run
when the lamp
is burned
down low   you baked
as you worked
broke (a dime
never stayed
in your pockets)
raised their children
loved sometimes
your own
(old lonesome road)
while Lincoln (bless
his ol'
soul)   is still thinking
run nigger run

Frederick Douglass

The slave
is a book
the Negro talking
    but not a poet writing
    sings
    the crust
the lash
    the fist
the man
Negro
free
    man
Freed Douglass
    his life
    in his fist *The Negro Sings A*
New Heaven

Annals of the Poor

I came to the Communist Party, with Bessie Smith, Marx and Garvey on my mind. I had known the third degree, death row, the back rooms of local police stations, shotgun in one hand, book in the other, firm in my resolve to stand up for my people. I joined the party in '35, year of the black storms; our freedom like something blowing in the trees. I was despondent as dusk, full mouth; lips like a thick slice of folded liver, grim as the blackness which was my father's face, as unfortunate as the children of Ham, who laughing at their father's nakedness, became what my father called the "cursed race." I am (like my father) a brute broad of mouth, sagging eyes, a back of muscle bent through work, and terrible posture, less a man, more a mule. A cruel man called Mississippi, made terrible by life, named after the awful river. Life like the angry Mississippi was the death and destruction of Negro song, in the flood uprooting houses and trees tearing through the community the lives of its useless people. My father was a man of harsh words and fierce anger. In my blood the darkness, the temper of my father flows, but in my head the words the thoughts of something gentle and unforgiving as the intellect of my mother. I came to the party my mother's son with a word on my lips, "Fight." Fight Nigger and fight she did and here I come because my mother was a woman fighting, a woman whose life was her sons and my father. I came to the party, a fist, a mind a man, I came because there was nowhere else to go.

Sweet Tooth

So black   so blue   Jelly
Roll is his sweet
tooth   & invisible too
this Hero
(name this man and his
mouth)
grin so wide
and white "cause my
teeth are pearly" (they
call me Shine)
of Ellison   who knew
Bessie Smith and Bigger
(nigger) T(om)homas the Brave
man with a sword   Booker T.
each thang kills
what he wants (not loves)
but Satchmouth plays (his music bugs
your inner eyes
like an insulting name)

for his mouth
(so white of teeth   and full
the grin is (like a great day
in the morning)
Louis
Armstrong so black so blue
Jazz on
Beale Street is Africa to me
old
sweet song
Satch mouth shine
not Martin or Malcolm
but the minstrel
of the black land wide grinning
(That old black music)
Louis Armstrong
speaks for me

Renters

Their feet knock
the floor
the bathtub gurgles
the windows brittle
and the water runs gray
and thick   but what I hear
is the landlord's
got the blues

Folks Like Me

In the unemployment line
with those early morning
economic blues
at home
on my feet   the president
said the economy is doing fine
(guess it's just taking its time getting
down   to folks like me)

What Can (Blind) Lemon Do?

Blind Lemon
born blind   music
in his fingers
sitting all afternoon
singing
to the darkness   all
afternoon
singing
talking
singing
cocky in his Stetson hat
said
(me & my guitar
makes ev'rything all
right) a fat man
picking
for my liquor
my women (fine meat shaking
on the bone)
on the sidewalks
my guitar & me
my mind rolls on
    that
blind man
sang so black
and blue
put it all
together
picking
that only Mr. Lemon
can do

Elegy

My father knew we were afraid and he was also afraid so that night after dinner, he brought a chair from the kitchen, put a shotgun across his lap and rocked back and forth & was cold because the sun went down early and the blackness of the woods around us made the world seem still and I felt like a young boy that everything was going to last forever because my father was outside our house ready to fight to protect myself, my mother and younger brother. I have wondered why I have not heard much about men like my father instead of those songs that sing why do you treat me so . . . my father was not a good man seldom home and mean to my mother and short-tempered with his sons. But he was that night the father I remembered sitting on the porch because he heard a Negro had talked back to some white man in town.

Hard Times

White
men in breadlines   soup
kitchens feed
America
the KKK
said break a few
collarbones
burn a few corn cribs and smoke
houses
let the white man
        speak

Landlord You're Wearin' the Door Out

Landlord you're wearin the door out
coming North is not what it should be but
some of us did dream
I boarded a steamship
to Harlem
saw Negroes
everywhere wanderin 'bout
worn out
Jesus leavin
town
every Sunday
Jesus in small
storefronts
blacker
than the night
over
the farm
Jesus   saving
125th Street
getting
down
& wasted at The Apollo
landlord
at my door
I think
of all the folks
back
home
sitting to supper
& all the days
and all the shoes
I am going to shine

Drinking A Hard Work Day

Music and a little moonshine
the day for me is almost done
but
my boss is standing   gray
above the everlasting sun so give
me a drink to wash my troubles
down

Unemployment Line Blues

1.
The ship
yard
s
shut
down
rent day
s
coming
I got
those
shut
down
blues

2.
I had
a brown
skin
woman
to hug
kiss
me
all
the time
a fine
woman
now
she can't
be found
lives
on the other
side
of town
those
low
down
no
jelly roll
blues

Blues Let Me Tell You

Rambling
blues
walking
in my bed
this morning
mean
things
in my head
blues
sitting
in my room
get
out
blues
troubling
my mind
I have a woman
can't
put her down
she's
a fever
in my
arms
she is
my lover
satisfies
a mind
living
in
this mean
as
a bull
frog
town

Meat

Willie Peterson's
mother believed
he would be president
Willie Peterson
ribs cooking
in the electric chair
Willie Peterson
Negro

The Lincoln Brigade

Fighting the nigger-hating
North old men (we are)
of the Lincoln Brigade
World War One vets
home to fight
again
Negro
men boys
of the South
those southern trees
bear strange
fruit   olden days
just inching away
we Negro Communists
(eyes screaming)
grinned
walk-in
the picket line before you
were born
fighting the nigger-hating
North

Negro Communists

When white
workers find
hotel rooms
the Negro worker
hits the street

Negro Communists 2

Wondering
about a bath
smellin like the workin
man I am
black skin
(smellin like
a hog
they say)
where can a Negro
brother
worker
sleep

Forever Robeson

I remember my father, our southern fathers, our Negro fathers. They taught me to say, "yes sir," but what they felt (meant) was not, "yes! sir" but of ourselves, their sons and daughters. I remember my father in his death. I never will regret knowing him. He died while I was passing out leaflets in Harlem, scrambling up the stairs and banging on doors, demonstrating in parks and city squares, talking about the world that was going to be made by workers. I remember my father and that he said, "someday," because he is in me and the cause of the worker. When I read Marx I thank my father. In these 1950s when we confirm or deny our politics, turn our backs on our brothers and fellow workers in the struggle, the name Paul Robeson is bitter to my lips. His great voice rang out, "I am going to keep fighting," like Old Man River, forever Robeson. This day Ben Davis sits in jail and rots. I think of my father and know all is not over but is only part of a long beginning.

Dusk Song for the Brown Bomber

A credit to his race in the ring
he was mean as a town where a Negro could
not let the sun sit on him
mean as a Texas sun
the Brown Bomber stepped
into the ring

in the shacks
in the tenements he made the people down and out holler like a
rhythm and blues song   when the Brown Bomber
a credit to his people knocked them
out   my English teacher (who taught all subjects with a ruler and a
mean demanding eye)
loved him as much as Paul Lawrence Dunbar   Dusk Song for the
Bomber
how 'bout some chitlins
for Joe (they stink worse than feet but's good eatin)
Some hog meat for Joe   made real fine.

His Fingers Seem To Sing

In the South
where I was born   color
bars and Jim Crow cars
fine brown-skinned girls
sang and black men danced
in their dark faces rolled

the merry and dangerous
whites of their eyes
I was young and made my
music beating
on hat boxes
my blues were color blind
and I traveled with my gin
a quart of whiskey a day
and ice across a country black
and white played drums on the streets
where policemen walked in groups
of fours and Fats Waller sat
at the piano
his fingers seemed to sing
and so did black America
through rural towns with moonshine
and poor whites
riots and thoughts of war
the music was swing and radio was the voice
that brought us together
my music was color blind
for fine young men in zoot suits
and brown skinned girls

Tap

(for Honi Coles)

We danced
      hard
      on the street soft
in the big
homes
of
millionaires   we did
our
     job
making it

Harlem Is the Place of Joyful Negro Song
or, Trying to Understand Gershwin's Good Intentions

Gershwin (can you believe it?) composed
Porgy and Bess but Harlem was the place
of endless song
Home for northern Negroes and the sadness
called the blues

poet laureate
Langston Hughes   poet of Negro joy
Church and Baptist sent
poet of a place called Uptown
laughing loving never singing those Dixie blues

Deep Chocolate

(for the Ink Spots)

Colored
boys:
sounding like the
sweetest chocolate
colored boys
long legged
colored boys
brown skinned boys
no good ever
loving
bowlegged
colored boys
home boys smelling
soul
food
jail birds
mama's boys good
boys
with bad   &
greasy
mops (swaying
to a little
be-bop
black boys writing
black
southern
black boy
shining
like
fine Sunday
shoes

Street Song

Freedom train
freedom train
ride here

on the
avenue
just my bottle and me

Apricot Bright and Tan

The sleeping car porters
Negro
men on the railroad
some were doctors
    lawyers
shining
    black
their faces miles of white
teeth so beautiful brown and black
tan and apricot bright like bananas
skin like baked potato smiling years of serving
    from Alabama to Baltimore
    believed in the church of Jesus
white Baptists and
    black

Sewer

In Harlem
(Negro capital)
not a
cot in this hotel
is worth
a dime

Strong

Strong
Sterling Brown
man
reading
Strong
Black man
reading
could have been a white
man
when he came
to town
a Joel Chandler
Harris
instead of a low
down blues
poet
with a piano player
throwing
a few licks
like a darkie
in a honky
tonk
strong men said
his deep voice
strong men
listen
to the music
the voice of Sterling
Brown
strong
man reading

Black is a Negro Full of Speeches

The Negro
worker   the working class
what did they
know of spoon bread
deacons
and shine
hard luck all
over town   dirty
work just to
keep going
northern cities
like
some white towns
talking
like Delta crackers
of coal town
nigger town
lonesome road
what do they know
of Negro song

Thoughts of a Georgia Boy

For Our Fathers

Harlem (he says) here I am
strutting down 125th with a
      walking stick
proud Negro
(black before Malcolm X
washed the conk from his hair)
with a handkerchief in his breast
pocket
old age (not a Georgia cracker) will get me down

Marcus Garvey   To Be a Negro

Name steamships Phyllis Wheatley
and Booker T. Washington
start the colored down the road
        is more than trying
to get orchestra seats
some of us read
the
Messenger (black voice and only the paper is white)
but others are way down
in Dixie (with that evening sun
sitting like the cracker
on our backs)

living
in New York
it's not
hard to
  understand Ol' Joe

Scottsboro Boy

                    Nineteen-thirty is forever
            in this state
where the law (makes a good nigger) is six months
    on the rock pile
we were just boys
on a slow moving train
in this county
if you don't have (Mr.) Charlie
            you are going to die
            I wrote to the president
            (we were just boys
on a slow moving train) in this state
            I am going to fry
yours truly
    a Scottsboro boy

but Mr. Roosevelt replied
            let the people
            of Alabama decide

in this state where the law
            is a white man
            the chair will make a good man out of me

The Talented 90%

When I met   (after riding
the Jim
   Crow
car wearin no
good clothes and smellin
   like a mule)   W.E.B.
he barely
lifted
his high yellow
   head

Spring 1931

Northern black
boy traveling
with empty belly;
these are the American
blues,
shanties, and fine
big houses, a sad
song
on a poor man's tongue
land of cotton and trouble
night sweet as dusk
on its gentle people
until today,
when
Scottsboro
was just a place
where the train
had to stop
and the Southern
night
was beautiful
I traveled
hungry
from Memphis to Georgia
drinking my whiskey
and
singing my blues

Negro Hero in *Ebony* Magazine
or, *Life* Magazine for the Black Bourgeoisie

Fought
the wars
in the kitchens of the navy
the quartermaster   & the
tank corps
fought the strike breakers
my father
(Negro hero
in our home)
once sang over there   over
there   over there   the Yanks
are coming
and my Negro friends
"lift every
voice"
my Negro friends
dead
in the South land
huddled
together in the northern
ghettoes
shunned
in the histories
taught
in her public schools

Claude McKay

Truth
is the fire
of *Banjo*
like the Hebrew
Moses
staff and sword
breaking
through the darkness
like
a new morning

I Married A Communist

In the fifties when I returned home from the service I saw the film *My Son John*, which was about Communism. In the film Robert Walker was effete, hated sports, was unkind to his mother and was slapped with a Bible by his god-fearing father who was a member of the American Legion. Whatever led men and women black and white to communism and social change was being questioned and condemned. In the film those who had been hunted by the black shirts the Klan and white supremacy groups were now subject to arrest by the government.

Picket Lines and Rubber Hose Wherever I Go

Paul Robeson
big and black—a voice
of Negro trouble:
fascist in Spain
and Russian war
relief   7 Jews
unwilling (Ethel and Julius give us back our
atom bomb) to be American or unable
to be of ropes and slums and Negro death
Paul Robeson sang "no hidin place" there
is a man some say J. Edgar Hoover
"takin names"
a past (were you there)
ask the deep bass
(J. Edgar was)
thought my father
but my mother knows
(when Negroes
were causes
and big black things)
and picket lines
and Paul Robeson
a friend
a voice   singing deep
river   there is a river
    called
    Jordan
    I am going to keep
    on fighting
    Paul Robeson
        is a man Mr. Hoover a Negro
singing "America"
a Negro going South
in my soul

Are You Now or Have You Ever Been

I hear America listening at the other end of the phone
America
is listening to the Jews
the Communists hugging
the Negroes   America is counting
her Jews
telling her Reds
to testify
to confess
her
intellectuals to burn
her writers
to think

Ebony

My father labored
in the mine his
hands blacker than
his face
face as black
as
coal   his hands
darkest
coal dust
my mother
a fair skinned
woman   former
schoolteacher
worked at home
read the Bible
and prayed &
I became
a communist

Robert W. Lee
A Friend

My father mistrusted
me   I was a godless
man   a Communist
walking
for the Scottsboro boys   even
rode the   rails
like them
I knew
the ghettos   recalled the light
dimming in the   prison tower
       the brave dark
       woman wife
       of Sacco & Vanzetti   Ethel &
       Julius Rosenberg
the painful words
of dead
men/women   whose peasant
lives became a cause
       my church is a worker's
       grave my bible
these papers
of the people
written by
those unaudited men:
       Black Kettle
       the railroad men
       the coal men
       the steel men
       and the Jew
       men from the fields
       the unskilled
       from the jails
       and prisons
       my brothers
       in the electric chairs
       hanging by
the neck   long
after death
on a southern road

Life Has Kicked Me
(On getting my first subpoena)

It is the fear
of
newspapers
a few dollars
in my pocket
thinking of life
in flop houses
America
thinks it is okay
strikes &
the cops
breaking
strikes in Detroit
the workers
heads broken
by the cops
offers made to kill
strike leaders
those times led many
like me
to seek change
through the gun
the ax handle
the meeting
in the basements
of bookstores
and living
rooms

To Howard Fast

Another Jewish boy afraid
of J. Edgar Hoover pounding
on his door   another Jew writing
hope is Lenin   intellectual
thought red and black
raised
Jewish in
Brooklyn
my father unwavering
as a man
liberal as a Jew

on his streets
I fought the Irish
street gangs (as did
the Negroes
fight)

fought
my father's bitterness
his anger the words of the Jews
the Christian stumbling block
the black man

my father taught me
truth he said whipped
and made a man out
of Howard Fast

Howard Fast's
heroes
step out
of the cities
the smoky
cities
of factories and brutal cops
collars pulled up
against the sharp winds

the bright lights
of hard
cities
and their men
I remember him
as he went to jail
as I think
of myself facing
America in the fifties

Historical Novelists
Those Indian Dead

I wrote first
the white man's
language about
the Red
man

          Comanche
          Nez Pierce

his loss
of land

          Bitter Root Mountains
          Walloa

and people

          Sand Creek
          (Wounded Knee

so much like my own
in Europe)

          Auschwitz
          Babi Yar

those Indian dead
in the Americas of black men
and Jews
marching in Washington
an American

          Goodman   Schwerner
          Cheney &   Till

in the Mississippi
red the blood
shed
in her wars   & rivers
just and unjust   white
her people
white an enemy
my race my country
tired of these

I write:

> *The Unvanquished*
> *The Passion*
> *of Sacco and Vanzetti*
> *The American*
> *Citizen Tom Paine*
> *The Proud*
> *and The Free*

Now I am another Jew
afraid of the man
pounding
upon my door

Black Bolsheviks I Have Known

These men hunted
like
Bigger Thomas
Stago Lee
David Walker
writing
summoning
Negro slaves
to war
Marcus Garvey
preaching Negritude
Sojourner
struck down
by Truth
slaughtered
like Bessie
and left
to die
with no
songs from their lives
like those spirituals
that
shook the soul
of Frederick
Douglass (remembered in February
cold month of presidents
and bitter winter)
I have known
these men their lives
and not their souls (who
led me to Communism) white men
and boys standing by Sacco and Vanzetti
the Scottsboro boys
marching
for the poor
the workers of the line
the factories
to Mississippi   mourning

Emmett Till
they marched
against Washington
and the war
found truth in economics
revolution
but most of all they
found me
in my ghetto
and forgotten inner
city
sang my blues
published
my poems
listened
To Harriet Tubman   Frederick
Douglass
told those
stories of the Negro
people
without
cruel laughing
of Joel Chandler
Harris
for them
yearned to read
became a Negro
Communist
from Harlem
and in jail
write these poems
to you

I Had Negro Friends . . .

who said that the niggers were happy doing their shuffling and jiving, drinking wine and getting welfare and King had to come along stir things up. I tell you something John said to me. John was 5'5" and full of opinions and all of them had to be told to your face with spit flying (John's mouth was a slop bucket of tobacco, spit, coffee, etc.). "A nigger ain't shit," was what he had to say most of the time. John's father was a taller man, 5'9", and used to beat up on John's mother. He was now a widower coming over (a little tipsy) to talk to the grandchildren and give his son advice on how to handle women. John did not like his father except that he at least knew how to keep his mother in line.

My memory of John is John with a dust pan. Smiling, I thought maybe he had just slapped his old lady, "Cat Bones." A kitten had wandered into the basement and John had lifted it up by the tail and swung it into the open furnace saying, "fucking cat." John hated everything and everyone, except me. I was reading all of the people he wanted to talk about and write like. John saw himself as the Negro Hemingway. He could not believe this shit I was reading (Faulkner, Himes). I was a smart motherfucker, weird and stinking, shoes coming apart and hungry all the time, one hundred pounds of b.o. He would talk to me and I would listen and he let me talk, and he would listen. He loved Langston Hughes and began to write poetry and short stories. John decided to read (he started with the *Fountainhead* and *Mein Kampf*), and after a while he stopped. There were no "niggers" writing. His wife did her housework, picking up John's drawers, shirts, socks (after they were smelling and entering the first week of wear), cooking dinner, which he ate and despised: "what is this shit?"—"Hemingway!, why don't you fuck him and be done with it," she screamed over dinner, called him a faggot from the second floor, calling me a faggot on Druid Hill Avenue. A lot of black men were reading, and listening to the opera on Saturday afternoons. That day John kicked open the door, twisted her arm; put his M-1 rifle into her mouth, and told her if she said just one motherfucking word he would kill her.

Homegrown Nigger #1

Thinking with his M-1 (red meat
lives in this nigger
body)
instead of the bar
the bottle
the hip
black world
or thinking
NAACP Negroes
this is me   my gun
no deep river
or camel hair
coat   (chopping up furniture
speaking in tongues
angry bullshit)
cheap wine
stumbling talking
on the pavements
my gun
is my word
a resolution)
instead of
the music   the blues
is a man walked on
& a slave's death
is the natural way
to go

Home Grown Nigger #2

John on fire   smoke billowing
thought:
the speech of white people
is their anger   and
    a cup of coffee
he drank in Georgia   smoking
and the whites hung
together
in nineteen-fifty
John's hair made straight
by grease and stocking
cap looking
at white people slurping
coffee
from a small
room for coloreds
called for other
than sweetness
he stood in line
burgers and fries
long tired lines
feet worn out
thinking
soldiers travelers
children—
Martin Luther King, Jr.
brings us
all to our feet
Georgia
Atlanta
Emmett Till
blues and church
bring Negroes
to their feet
those Southern songs still able
to move the spirit   move
the feet
make the hands clap   summon

their anger
like Baptists
Christ to the darkness
of the church

Negro preacher
walking
his word
to fire
in the Bible
his blood
to life

John's Poem:
We Are Brothers
& Talk That Way

All my life
I (bad feets &
kidneys
evil
women
black as
homemade sin)
have been
a man   to punch
you out
clean your
clock   even
the Baptist church
don't fuck with me   for my
people   I love
Negroes being one
but that don't mean
a nigger
ain't shit (to me)

living like hogs
shooting
crap

but this Nigger
has done
more
with his mouth
and say lawd lawd
yes sir no sir

The Negro has been
Langston Hughes
the history
of the Negro
is the river
in Africa
the Ohio (cross

over   cross
over)
the Mississippi
no wonder I love
the Negro sneaking
and jiving   acting
like a fool

pullman on the railroad
car giving
food to the hungry
from the kitchens
to the hungry in the cities
to the sad children
of the streets
the rent money

sorry Stokely
too bad
Malcolm

some of us
have been men
long before you
were
Red peddling
whores
dancing like a jig
straight hair
burned across your
head of Dixie peach
(who do you think
you are Cab Calloway)

let me put my brothers
down we are
family
talk that way

cause we love each other
this talking nasty (you guys)
is just speaking
in tongues
like a man of God

Long Hair God Almighty Nappy Hair

Thank god I got (although it don't
move when the wind blows) good hair/bad hair
but Michael Jackson does not
believe it nor did Nat
King Cole
blackness is a music
planting the blues about how God
(and men) have done me wrong
let me down
with a hundred curls
upon my head
thousands make the dusk of
Africa there
God give (and gave me and some
of us) this hair forever nappy and long

Almost Gone

I think
of the folks
and home
and lift
my tired and broken
feet
with a song
from
a weary throat
that blesses the sun
creates
the thirst
and fire
I sit down
a spell
then rest
and feed
for another
day is getting
ready to come

From Our Terrible Heart

Not a Christ but a Moses
once a proper   darkie   eager
to dance   to leap
for candy and a pat
upon the head   proud
of the printed words I read
and knew as Gospel
from the page
to my lips
God's bloody words
rising like a river

but still I pulled
the cotton
sowed the seed
slept on the floor
and waited for the word
the heavens   to open
when it did
I Nat Turner took up the sword

and freedom
the beatings the madness   the word made flesh
from our terrible hearts   not a Christ but a Moses
with thunder   and the sword   to lead
            my people
this proper darkie (I Nat Turner)   this black
and horrible man ready
to make   war   to slaughter
whites   like beast   and fowl

Blues (A Christian Fundamentalist Speaks)

A Negro
woman looking at a black
   man
watching a yellow woman
with a body that ought to be locked up in the county jail
   blues
a policeman
   armed with
an eviction notice
   blues
black
mayor Wilson Goode sixty row houses a tunnel that is a basement
blues
   a black neighborhood thinking
   it is middle class
picking up the phone
   dialing 911

James Baldwin

Fire in the city   and Malcolm
has no pity   Bigger Thomas   this
is the threshing floor meet
your terrible maker   Uncle Tom
spent and wasted   father burnt
out like a Harlem full of anger
fire make me a world this time

Emmett Till (August 1955)

If the South was a woman he would whip it into shape
the South
was hell for him
because he read
about
it   heard about
it all
of his life
Negroes sitting
in backs of buses
bags of food
in their laps
bladders tight
in silence sweating
bladders tight
fuck
the South (as if it were
his wife)
he said spitting
on the floor
on Negroes for sitting
black faces
King moved to
anger (instead of work
off the welfare
rolls) back
to church
full of collard greens
(a little Allah
thrown in)
now where were they
when Lady Day
crept
into a nigger grave

laughing
at Marcus Garvey
(wanting
to kick his big
black ass)
fuck the South
but
never Emmett Till

1953

My niece was a little girl doing what little girls do: going to school, and what little girls should never have to do: suffer. What is historical for us is common for white people.

My niece small brown girl hair in tails, pulled tight, greased tiny lips, brown eyed thin legs walking in white socks, blue dress dark dress, clean as washing can make it, bright as new clothes can be fresh and full of life as she enters school, unlike me who walked to a one-room school where a Negro teacher taught. A school named for our father, our savior, our misguided man of education Booker T. Washington. I read his book *Up From Slavery* and saw how far we had come from slavery's door to finding this school (where I was a student). He was writing books and telling them (white people) how we can be equal in all things and separate; that is, segregated. For him we were in school all black and cold in the winter with books about to fall apart in your hands. But Booker saw the world gathering about Negro Americans as it did the Indians (who once covered this land like the forest) in a world when once animals were more than men, and women a little less than animals, with an angry God, who spoke through John Brown, Harriet Tubman and Nat Turner's sword and then at last quietly, through the Supreme Court.

Sleeping So Long the Bus Boycott

was tired   Negro feet   working women all day
how long   justice just takes its time
on their feet   these women   they speak
my mind   before morning and late at night
walking   these women tired arms and feet   white men heard only
niggers stumbling to their feet
(after sleeping so long)

Half A Negro

My mother was one of the most beautiful women I have ever known. Half Negro, one quarter Indian, another quarter white (my grandmother was a mulatto). Her hair was as dark as the wood where I expected to find Rose Red, Br'er Fox eyeing the gingerbread house. My mother's hair was like Debra Paget in *Broken Arrow* (Hollywood's Indian woman), long and flowing down the length of her back, her fine chiseled nose gave an air of irreverence unlike the women in the district. Some people wanted to give her a fat lip. My mother's face was a reddish pale brown. My father was a man of broad nose. Some call it corpulent, face with thick and abundant lips. His brown eyes were a brilliant white fire when he was angry. But my father was not a nigger, he was a man of God. The wrath that the Book demanded of those who took up the cross. He knew the fires of Hell were hot and eternal and so he fought sin, the devil in the cabin, the sin in the cotton fields, Satan, the demons of long nights in the weekend brawls, the burning slow death of moonshine, in my father's fist was the Word of God but in his heart was the fire that was the love of my mother.

Larry Neal

Black so Goooooooooooood Dead Black boy
sleeping like a chile
in a Dunbar
lyric
(or thinking
like Br'er Bear
he'd sleep all winter)
Larry Neal
one morning
the world's on fire
Detroit   Newark
Watts   black world's
smoking

dead black poets
Dunbar and Wheatley
wake up Langston man
black fire

Larry Neal (woke up
this morning feeling
black so Goooooooood
pen on fire

our song my poems
woke up this morning
writing
poems in my head

Larry Neal
black poet
on fire

Larry Neal
black fire

Since I Have Seen You

Something brought the men
of my generation
out of the rolling dark
southern towns
the cities   and rows
of tenement shacks where the names
of generations
of Italian   and Irish
names were written beneath
the wallpaper of the rooms
which stayed as they
moved on and
closed the cities against
us into north ends
little Italian   rows
of marble steps in Polish
ghettoes   in Baltimore

something from the labor
the lynchings and boss man
with their promises
and of work brought me
to Communism   white
boys talked of the people
living in boxcars with the promises
of Herbert Hoover

I knuckled around
the jails and towns
talked about my hard
times in the Baptist church
when the choir sang
help me cross the river
we ended
our song still on the other
side waiting for the
sun to shine waiting for
the word the presence

way in the middle
of the air   the promise of sorrow
songs held not the truth
of the white boys in the Communist
party   bringing me drunk
without a dime for this job
bringing my people the street
to march to strike

1960

      Stokely said   the war was declared by LBJ sending tanks into
Newark but a Negro had the match the Deacons the Panthers said
if you are a Negro you might as well be dead H. Rap Brown stood
      on top of a brother's car (ass against the window
feet on the hood spoiling the wash it took so many hours to do
      that Sunday)   Stokely said all that Negroes did
      with their mouths was say yes suh and stuff your face
      big boy angry mouth made the papers sell
      (and Negroes read) my old man knew when Rap
      came to Baltimore the city was going
down the church did not (could not) save Martin Luther King   Set
fire to a gas station sorry about King sorry about Malcolm   Sorry
about that four days let him down when the fires were out the
National Guard patrols the street we wondered where we were
going to stay   But Stokely would never rest
until his people were free.   This is war but somebody forgot to tell
the people

Ohio After The Shooting At Kent State
(June 1970)

We enter the mountains,
The sudden trees are quiet,
Moonlight finds stones and dust,
The bones of slow animals in the grass.

12/1/87

But when the dance is over
the music of the banjo
is slow
as a sinking sun
his day is done
and gone
step back step
back
turn his picture to
the wall
lift
up your glass
a toast to dusk
James Baldwin died
today
December 1, 1987

Robert Hayden

A Negro
almost yellow
a wave
in his hair
wrote
a formal verse
once cool
now an uncle (but just a
little while) once
wore a suit
offended
Booker T. Washington
& the brothers
who took to the streets
(kill the Pigs
leave them in little pieces)
those who shouted
burn
baby burn
but it is Hayden's star
burning
now

GLOSSARY

Note: The Glossary represents a partial list of historical and biographical information. It is a combination of these and the author's personal feelings and observations of these people and places.

Historical References

Louis Armstrong/Satchmo: Jazz trumpet player. Ralph Ellison referred to Louis Armstrong as one of America's cultural heroes in his novel *Invisible Man.* Mr. Armstrong, despite his success as a musician, was regarded as an "Uncle Tom," making him the subject of amusement and contempt in the black community.

Bigger Thomas: A fictional character and protagonist in the novel *Native Son* by Richard Wright. Such a violent character that Wright later apologized for his presence in the novel. Nonetheless, the archetype is a common character for authors and playwrights dealing with realism in drama and fiction.

Broken Arrow: Classic Hollywood western which attempted a more humane portrait of the American Indian. With James Stewart and Deborah Paget.

H. Rap Brown: A black militant of the 1960s–1970s. It was rumored that where Brown would go, riots would follow.

Sterling Brown: Will always be regarded as a poet of the Harlem Renaissance and Depression eras. Well known for his feeling for the blues/folk idiom.

Stokely Carmichael: Outspoken black leader of the 1960s who is held accountable by contemporary conservative historians for some of the political turmoil of that era. Obviously, Mr. Carmichael was merely a voice for the discontent and anger which surfaced at that time.

Honi Coles: Professional tap dancer who appeared in Francis Ford Coppola's *The Cotton Club.*

John Coltrane: Popular jazz saxophonist. Coltrane's jazz composition, "A Love Supreme," is a musical odyssey attempting to define unconditional love and is used as an underlying theme in the Spike Lee movie, *Mo' Better Blues,* which is a cinematic dramatization of Mr. Coltrane and his music.

Jim Crow (laws): "Ethnic discrimination esp. against the Negro by legal enforcement or traditional sanctions." (Webster) Originally from a 19th century vaudeville racial stereotype.

Benjamin Davis: African-American Communist who was elected to public office and was eventually incarcerated for his beliefs.

Paul Lawrence Dunbar: Son of slaves whose father escaped from the South via the Underground Railroad. Most successful black writer of the 19th century. Wrote novels and poems. Best known for his poetry in black Southern dialect (which we had to learn to recite in elementary school when I was a boy). Author of classic urban novel, *Sport of the Gods.*

Owen Dodson: Professor of drama at Howard University and artistic consultant to the Harlem School of the Arts. Novelist and poet whose work emerged briefly during the 1960s, although he was publishing poetry in the 1940s. A fine lyric poet in the tradition of James Weldon Johnson.

Frederick Douglass: One-time slave who wrote and rewrote his autobiography, consulted with presidents and abolitionists, an advocate of women's rights, was aware of the importance of Africa in the lives of Negro slaves. Perhaps the foremost African-American of his day.

William Edward Burghardt DuBois: One of the founders of the NAACP; editor of magazine *Crisis.* Author of essays, novels, poetry, autobiography, most influential book sold to black audience. Prominent works are *Black Reconstruction* and *Suppression of the African Slave Trade.*

Howard Fast: Highly skilled American popular novelist. Unlike most commercial writers, however, he saw American history as drama including people of all races, ethnicities and creeds. He was briefly imprisoned during the McCarthy era for his beliefs. His novel *Freedom Road* is a brilliant, romantic portrait of the post-Civil War era.

Marcus Garvey: Jamaican-born black nationalist who was always in deep trouble with other black leaders such as W.E.B. DuBois for his views and his mass appeal.

Wilson Goode: Mayor of Philadelphia who was held responsible for the bombing by the Philadelphia police of a militant organization called MOVE.

D.W. Griffith: White filmmaker who was often credited for solidifying the commercial cinema with his racist epic *Birth of A Nation*. His film and the philosophy of Booker T. Washington, ironically, co-existed for some time in America.

George Gershwin: American composer who was held accountable for alleged misrepresentation of Negro life and music in his celebrated opera, *Porgy and Bess*.

Joel Chandler Harris: White Southern writer responsible for one version of the *Uncle Remus* tales, of which Br'er Rabbit is a character. In a paternalistic way, he may be seen as a chronicler of African-American folk tales.

Angelo Herndon: Writer and American Communist, author of the book *Let Us Live*, a major black autobiography of the 1930s.

Chester Himes: Famous African-American novelist known for his mystery novels set in Harlem. Was of the Realist school, made prominent by novelist Richard Wright.

J. Edgar Hoover: Former director of the FBI. Reportedly kept records on everybody, especially prominent black Americans.

Ink Spots: Early black singing group. Most famous song, "I Don't Want to Set the World On Fire." Used to be lampooned on old television variety shows such as "Your Show of Shows."

Kent State: Incident involving the shooting of four students at Kent State University in Ohio. It was the turning point of the anti-war movement in America during the 1970s and to many Americans, represented the brutality of the American army toward young civilians.

Black Kettle: Native American, one of the chiefs of the Southern Cheyenne who attempted to make peace with white settlers. Nevertheless, in 1864, a charge led by Col. J.M. Chivington attacked and destroyed his village at Sand Creek.

Stago Lee: One of the apocryphal "bad niggers with high conscience." Cf. Richard Wright's character, Bigger Thomas.

Lincoln Brigade: Black volunteers in the Spanish Civil War.

Joe Louis (aka "The Brown Bomber"): Athlete and one-time heavyweight champion of the world. Role model for young black Americans during the 1930s–1940s because he was notoriously kind to his family, made plenty of money, and could punch out a white man in the boxing ring and wouldn't get lynched for it.

Claude McKay: Jamaican-American poet best known during the Harlem Renaissance. Also wrote novels. Best known for poem "If We Must Die," said to have been quoted by Winston Churchill facing the threat of Hitler on the eve of World War II. Created character named Banjo, a sort of free-spirit primitive.

The Messenger: Newspaper published by Marcus Garvey.

Pauli Murray: Born in Baltimore; first black Attorney General of California. Taught law at Yale and Boston University and one of the founders of NOW. Author of a book about her family history entitled *Proud Shoes*. Contemporary of many Depression-era writers.

My Son John: Of many anti-Communist films of the 1950s, *My Son John* was perhaps the most simplistic and reactionary. John the son is an "effete" intellectual and a "mama's boy." The father is a member of the American Legion who, at one point in the film, hits his son on the head with a Bible. The film would be regarded as ludicrous today, yet it depicts all the popular 1950s stereotypes of the intellectual.

Larry Neal: Co-editor with LeRoi Jones (Amiri Baraka) of *Black Fire*, a landmark anthology which first incorporated the new black writing of the 1950s and 1960s literary consciousness.

Haywood Patterson: One of the famed "Scottsboro Boys," who along with several other black boys, was in the 1930s convicted of raping and abusing several white women in a railroad car in the South. Haywood escaped prison and, along with Earl Conrad, co-authored the book, *Scottsboro Boy*, which was reprinted by Bantam Books in the 1950s.

Franklin D. Roosevelt/Eleanor Roosevelt: President and First Lady of the U.S. during much of the Depression and World War II. According to political historians (most recently, David McCullough, the author of *Truman*), Eleanor was regarded as the best-loved first lady of this century for her direct involvement in social causes, her intelligence and willing activism in social and racial issues. Within the standards of the period, Franklin appeared willing to accommodate Negro causes.

Paul Robeson: Actor, singer, writer, political activist. Career nearly destroyed by McCarthyism in the 1950s. Because of his communist affiliation, he was hounded by both blacks and whites. Made several films, the best known of which are probably *King Solomon's Mines* and *The Emperor Jones*. Also a Rhodes scholar. His voice can be heard on the soundtrack of Sidney Lumet's film, *Daniel*.

Ethel and Julius Rosenberg: Were tried and executed for treason during the Eisenhower era. Anti-Semitism and anti-Communism played a strong part in deciding their guilt.

Scottsboro Case: Famous incident occurring in the 1930s in Scottsboro, Alabama when several black men hoboing on a train were accused of raping and abusing some white women who were also hoboing on the train.

John Philip Sousa: The "March King," who composed "The Stars and Stripes Forever," still performed by the Boston Pops and other light classical repertory groups. His music was played by marching bands when I was a boy.

Sojourner Truth: Runaway slave who is best known today by American feminists for her statement, "I Am A Woman." Sojourner Truth's reputation has been somewhat overshadowed by that of Harriet Tubman, who was also active in the Underground Railroad, and who personally led many slaves from the South to the North.

Emmett Till: Fourteen-year old black boy thrown into the Tallahatchie River for allegedly whistling at a white woman. Body discovered in Mississippi in 1955.

Harriet Tubman: Abolitionist and runaway slave. Often known as "Moses" by historians and fellow abolitionists for her participation in the Underground Railroad leading Negroes North.

Nat Turner: Slave insurrectionist, leader of the best known and recorded slave revolt (1831). Little else is known of Turner's life. The controversy surrounding *The Confessions of Nat Turner* by William Styron, involved the depiction of Nat Turner as a tortured man with sexual visions of white women and questionable sexuality.

David Walker: Born in 1828 a free man in Wilmington, NC. Published *Walker's Appeal*, in which pamphlet he urged slaves to "kill or be killed."

Booker T. Washington: Author of autobiography *Up From Slavery*, advocate of agricultural education for the American Negro and held responsible by many for legitimizing segregation laws through his philosophy.

Phyllis Wheatley: Rumored to be first African-American to publish poetry. Better known as being "the first," rather than for the quality of her work. Critics praised her poetry because it was written by a Negro and therefore, considered nothing short of miraculous.

Walter White: Deceased Negro lawyer for the NAACP, 1940s. So fair of skin that he often passed for white in Southern towns.

Personal References

Eddie: Former family friend who was a surrogate stepfather.

John: Personal friend who lived in Baltimore, and reflected a common attitude toward the sit-ins and bus boycotts.

Robert W. Lee: Good friend, proprietor of the New Era Bookstore in Baltimore, a political bookshop.

Miss Sally: One of my mother's neighbors.

Miss Sarah: Another of my mother's neighbors.